The Organ Project

A coloring book and a basic introduction to organs of the Human Body & how they work as an Orchestra (3 years +)

Renee Grace

AuthorHouse™
1663 Liberty Drive
Bloomington, IN 47403
www.authorhouse.com
Phone: 1 (800) 839-8640

Published by AuthorHouse 05/11/2018

ISBN: 978-1-5462-3219-3 (sc)
ISBN: 978-1-5462-3221-6 (hc)
ISBN: 978-1-5462-3220-9 (e)

Print information available on the last page.

authorHOUSE®

Acknowledgements

Markia Armstrong RN; Jeanne Marino, Elizabeth Becker CPC, Marie Jackson, Patricia Holland, Kathi Gibbons, Asha Mandhare RN, Areica Graham, Dr. Marijo Wilson, Marilyn Mowen RN, all gave valuable input in this work:

Dedication:

this book is dedicated to all the children of the world as a blessing to bring health, honor, life and knowledge to cherish your body as the most valuable, beautiful gift you will ever receive.

You are a work of Art, from God, for you to take care of.

1 Corinthians 6: 19-20: "Do you not know that your bodies are temples of God, who is in you, whom you have received from God?

You are not your own: you were bought at a price.

Therefore, honor God with your bodies."

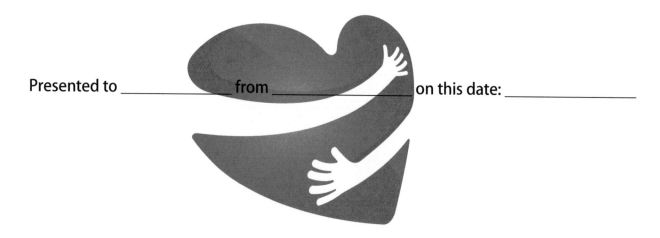

Presented to _____ from _____ on this date: _____

Jordans Story

Jordan was 5 years old when starting school as a vibrant, energetic, outgoing, curious child. Sleep was unimportant to Jordan and stayed up playing long after being put to bed.

One morning, upon awakening, Jordan was overcome with tiredness and unable to enjoy school, playtime or friends.

Then, one day while outside playing with mom, Jordan became so exhausted and tired, playing was no longer fun and had to sit down to rest.

Mommy Josephine, being a nurse, knew this was not normal for a 5 year old child and brought Jordan to the doctor.

Jordan was found to have a heart condition from exhaustion; not enough sleep.

Jordan, determined not to let this stop playtime and being with friends, made a strong decision to learn about the body and how to take care of it. After all, where is the heart? In addition, going to the doctor is NO FUN! Jordan started to learn.

Jordan went to the library and started a project named, **"The Organ Project"**.

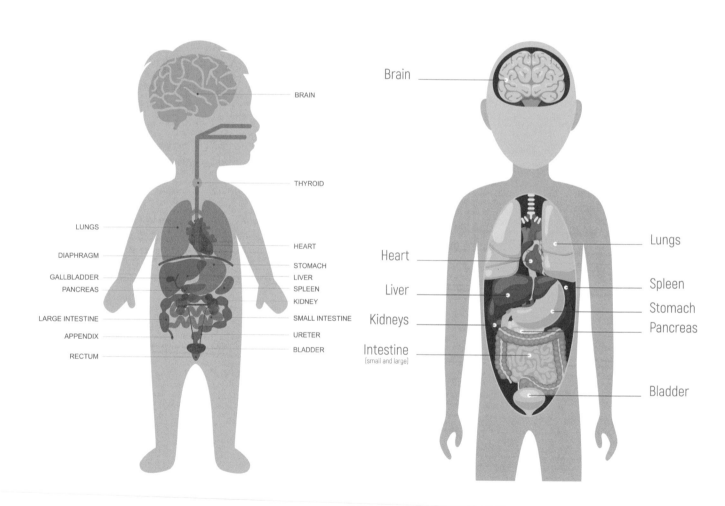

Jordan got a good picture what is inside the body. Heart, bones, stomach, blood and muscles all organized into different systems: they work together in harmony as an orchestra. Staying up late, the heart and other organs would not do A+ work without enough sleep.

Organs

Organs of our body: the brain, heart, lungs, stomach, colon, spleen, pancreas, liver and gall bladder. They depend on each other to work as a symphony.

Bones protect the inside of our bodies; the organs, tissues and blood vessels. It supports and is surrounded by the skin which is the largest organ.

When we eat, food goes through a process (digestion) to use for energy and helps our organs to work.

Blood moves through a system which is pumped from the heart. It brings oxygen and nutrients (that we get through food) through our body.

Muscles support our entire body to be able to stand, sit, play, dance, run and are attached to the bones.

HUMAN ORGANS THIN LINE ICON SET

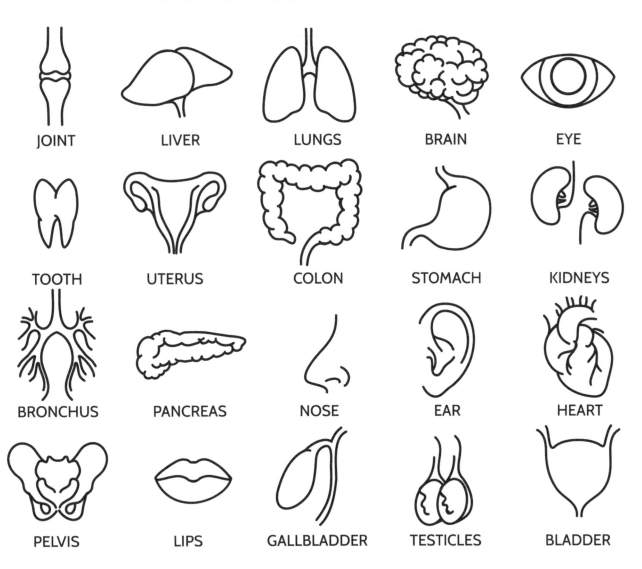

JOINT   LIVER   LUNGS   BRAIN   EYE

TOOTH   UTERUS   COLON   STOMACH   KIDNEYS

BRONCHUS   PANCREAS   NOSE   EAR   HEART

PELVIS   LIPS   GALLBLADDER   TESTICLES   BLADDER

Match and name the organs

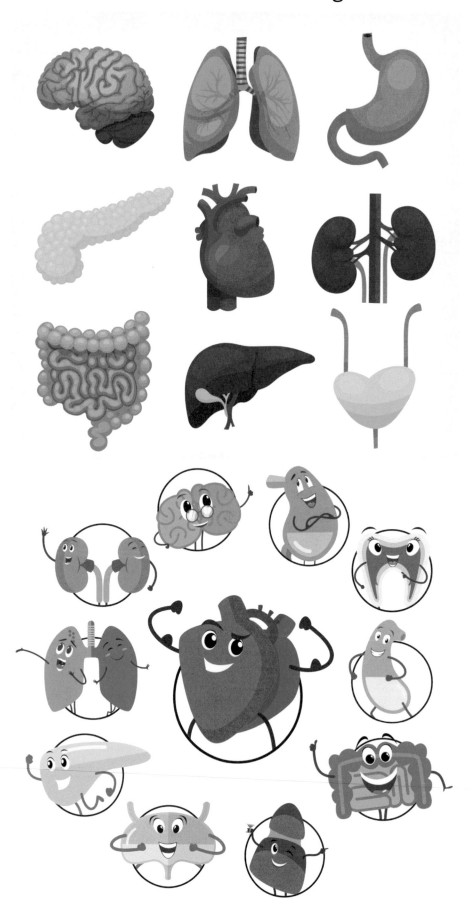

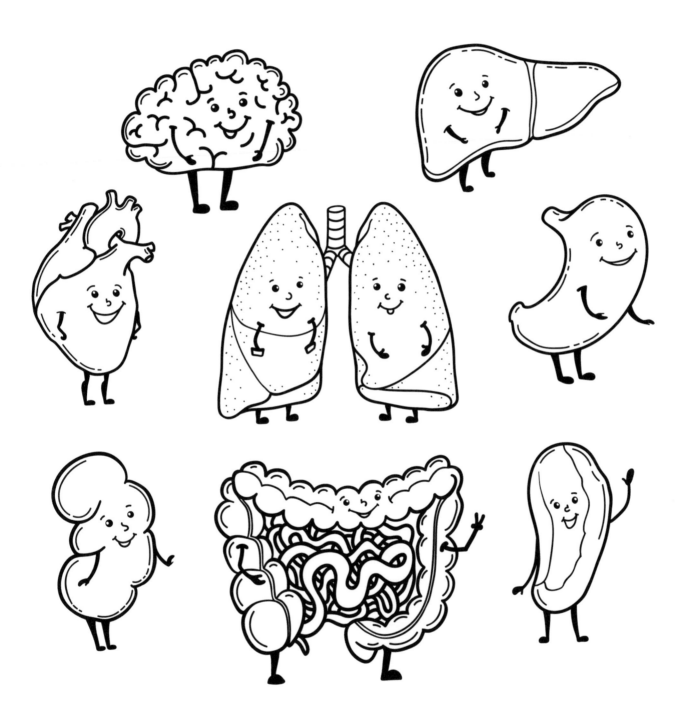

Brain

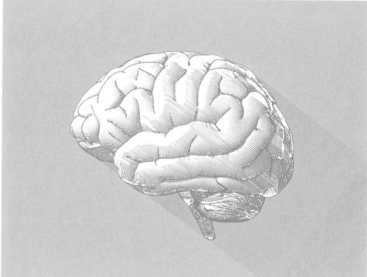

We go to school to help our brain learn. The brain tells us how to walk, talk, think, sing, draw pictures, color and play.

THE BRAIN is pinkish- beige in color.

Our brain tells our body how to work. It tells our organs, bones, skin, digestion how to work together.

Foods to feed your brain; eggs, salmon, meat, nuts and vegetables. Vegetables and fruit that grow from the ground, trees or bushes are best.

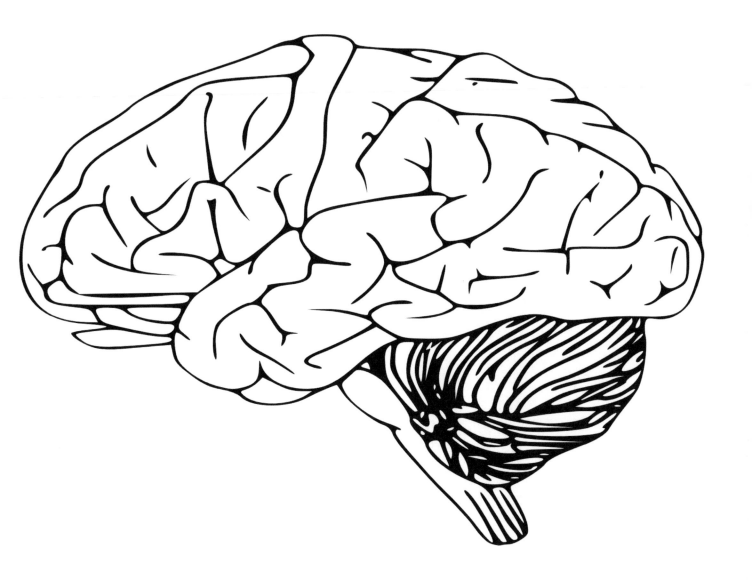

Eyes

Your eyes help you to see, read, watch TV, see danger.

People have different color eyes; blue, brown, green, grey.

Foods to eat: dark green vegetables, fish- salmon, avocado, carrots, eggs, berries and almonds.

Lungs

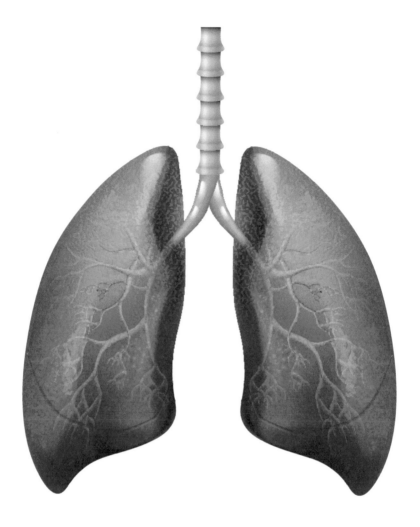

Your lungs are like two sponges when air moves in and out allowing you to breath. Fresh clean air is essential to healthy lungs.

Your lungs are pinkish at birth and darken as we get older.

Playing increases the amount of air that goes in and out of your lungs.

Blood picks up air in your lungs and moves through your blood producing energy to play.

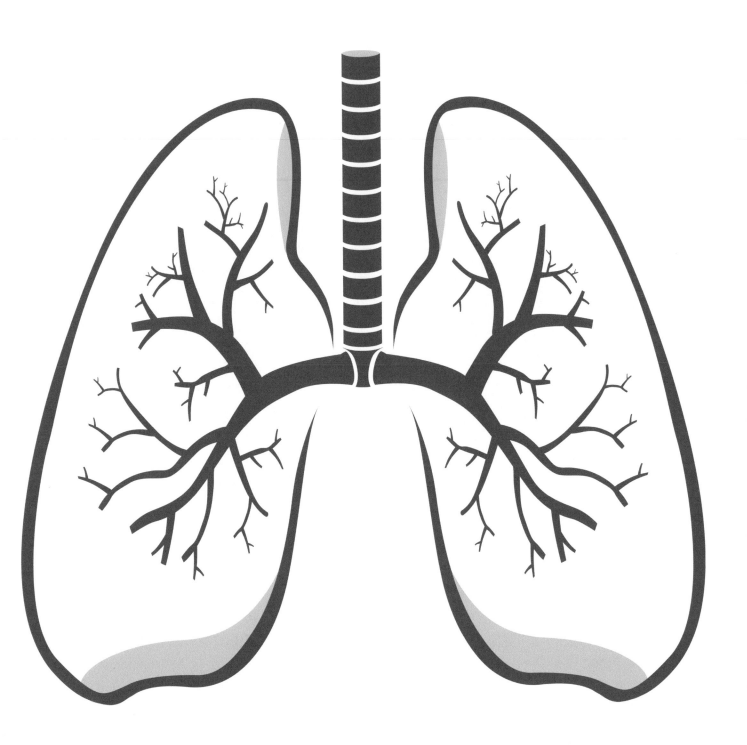

Heart

The heart pumps blood through your body and brings energy through air from your lungs. The heart pumps harder and gets stronger when playing.

Your heart is a hearty brownish red - red.

Food that is good for your heart. Meat, fish, dark green vegetables, chicken, berries, tomatoes, oatmeal.

Your Heart is one of the most important organs in your body.

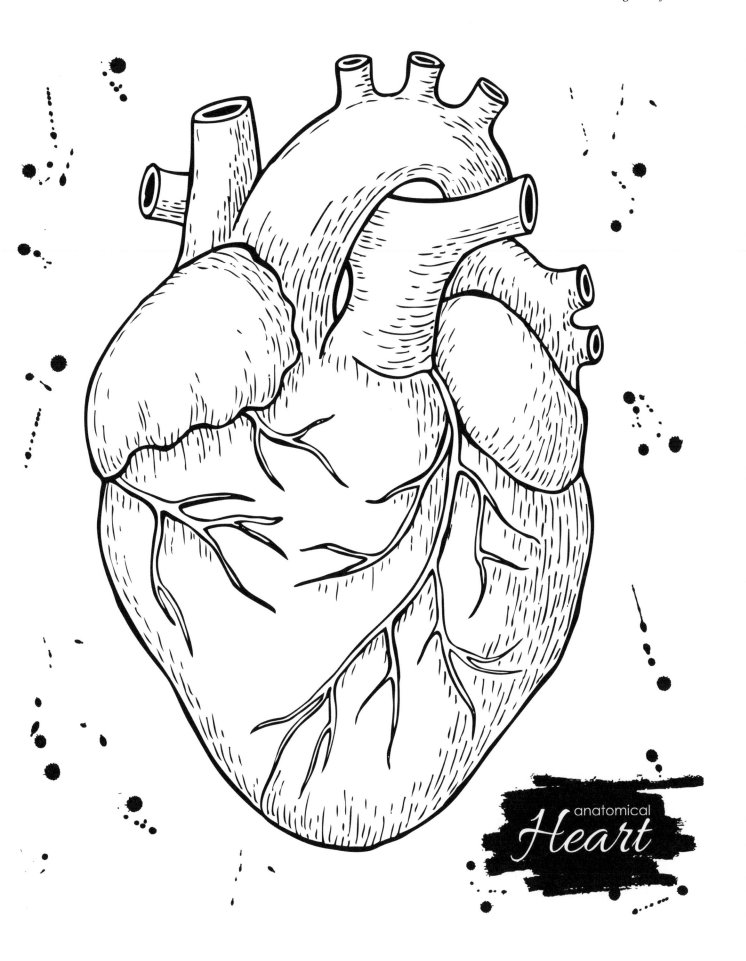

anatomical
Heart

Liver and Gall bladder

Human Liver Anatomy

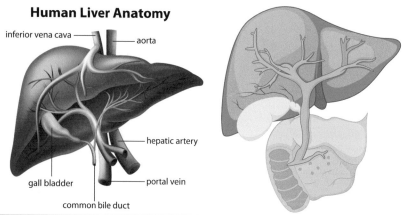

The liver cleans waste. It is important to eat food that is healthy, natural food. The liver also helps to manage nutrients we get from food.

The liver is brownish red in color.

Foods for your liver: garlic, beets, parsley, dark green vegetables, avocados, apples, lemons, grains, nuts and seeds.

The gall bladder has bile (a yellow brown liquid) made by your liver. The bile is sent to your intestine to digest fats from food we eat. The gall bladder itself is a green color.

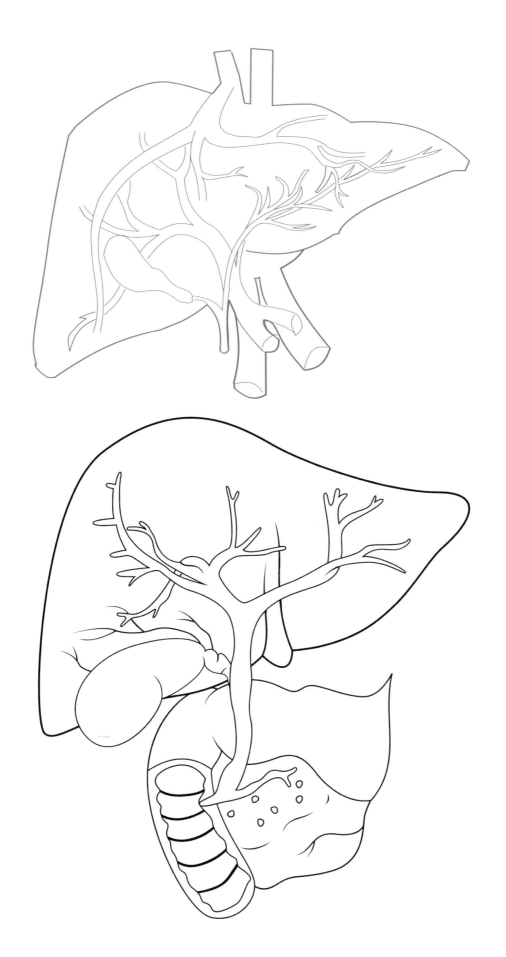

Pancreas

The pancreas sends enzymes and helps to stabilize blood sugar and maintain a safe environment for your blood. It also helps in digestion of food.

The pancreas is a tannish - pink - yellowish color.

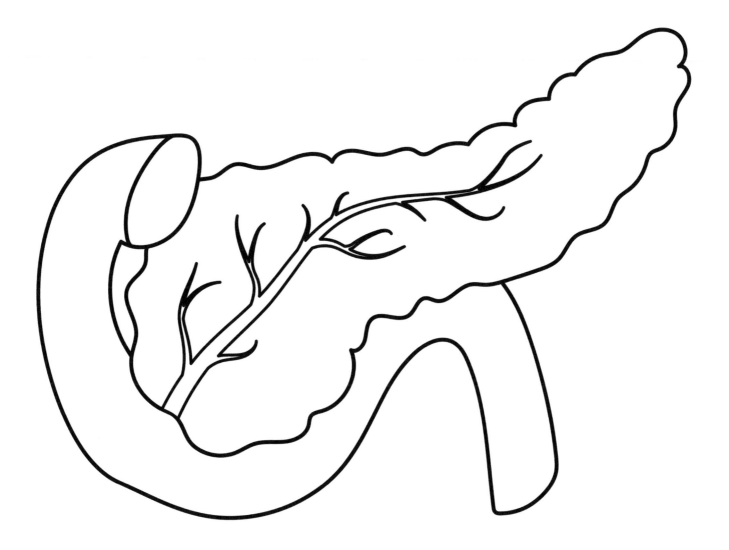

Spleen

The structure of the spleen

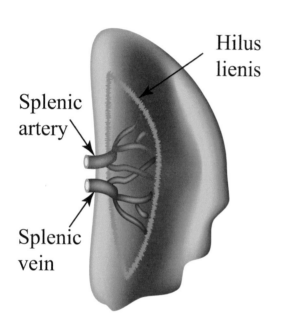

Hilus lienis

Splenic artery

Splenic vein

RED BLOOD CELLS

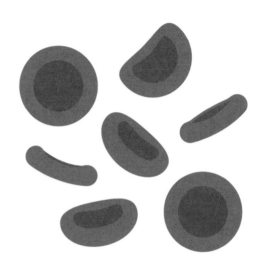

EPS 10

The spleen (brown in color) makes blood. It is important to eat meat to produce blood cells.

There are different kinds of blood cells made by the spleen. Red and white blood cells make up blood.

Leafy greens and root vegetables such as sweet potatoes are extra nourishing for your spleen. Carrots, rice, barley, squash, pumpkin, apples, ginger, garlic are all good for healthy blood.

Erythrocyte

Platelet

Leukocyte

Eosinophil

Basophil

Lymphocyte

Monocyte

Neutrophil

Kidneys

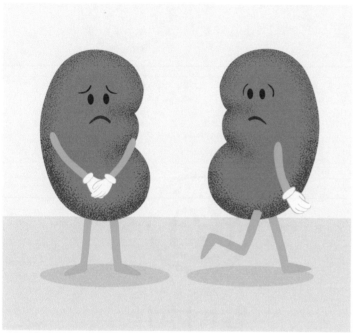
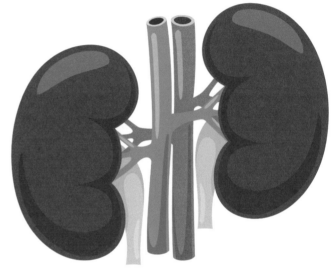

The kidneys clean waste from your body then goes to your bladder. The kidneys are reddish - browny.

When you feel full (need to go number 1) this means to listen to this urge and go to the bathroom right away.

It is important to drink clean water every day to keep kidneys clean.

Cranberries, and Asparagus are also good for your kidneys.

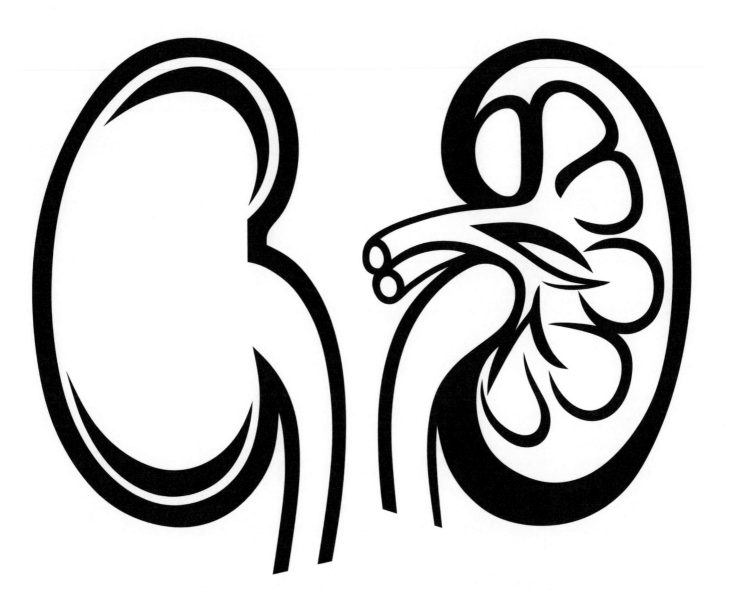

Bladder

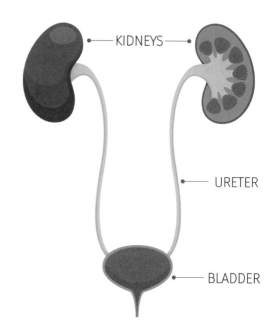

The bladder collects urine from the kidneys; this is when we have to go #1.

The bladder is hollow and pinkish in color.

Foods for your bladder; clean water, cranberries, lemon and oranges.

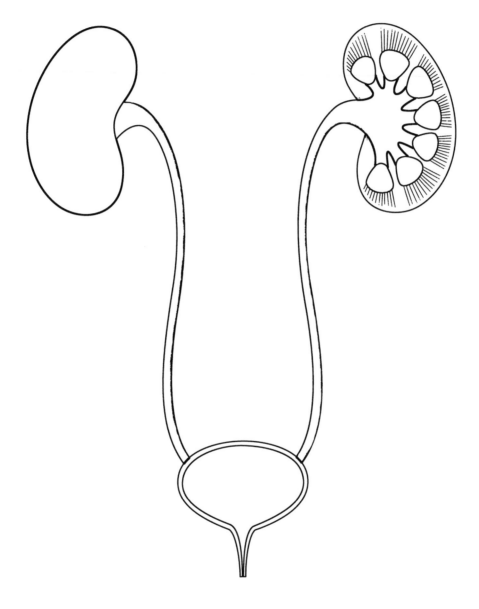

Stomach

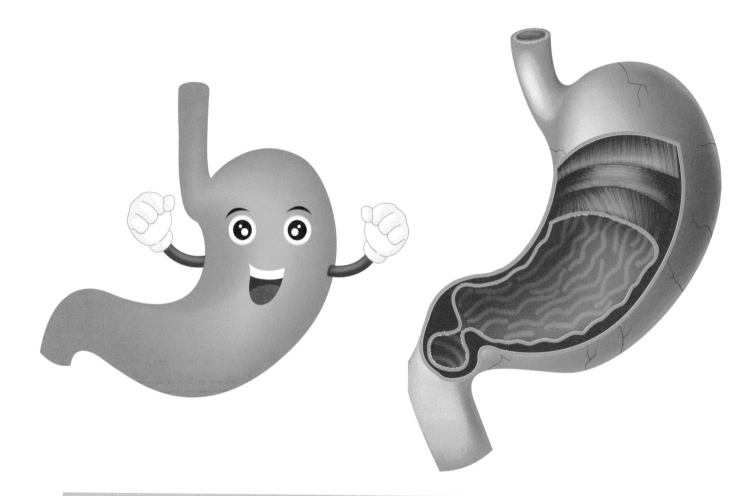

Food goes to your stomach when you eat. Enzymes churn up the food into a thin or thick liquid then moves to your intestine.

The stomach is a tan - light pink.

Foods good for your stomach are anything that comes from the ground, or fruit from trees, berries; meat, fish and chicken that are cooked well.

It is important to eat just until comfortably full.

Don't be a fat cat!

Intestine

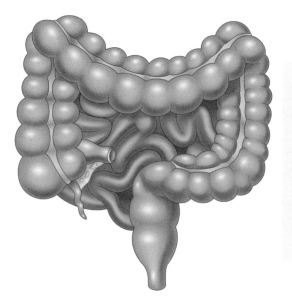

There is a small and large intestine; it is a long tube that processes food from your stomach when you eat. Vitamins and minerals absorb here. This is also where waste from food passes, then you must go number 2. This is a very important, normal part of life, and keeps you healthy.

The colon is a greyish - purple color.

Foods to eat. Vegetables, fruits, grains, nuts, yogurt.

Apples.

An apple a day keeps the doctor away.

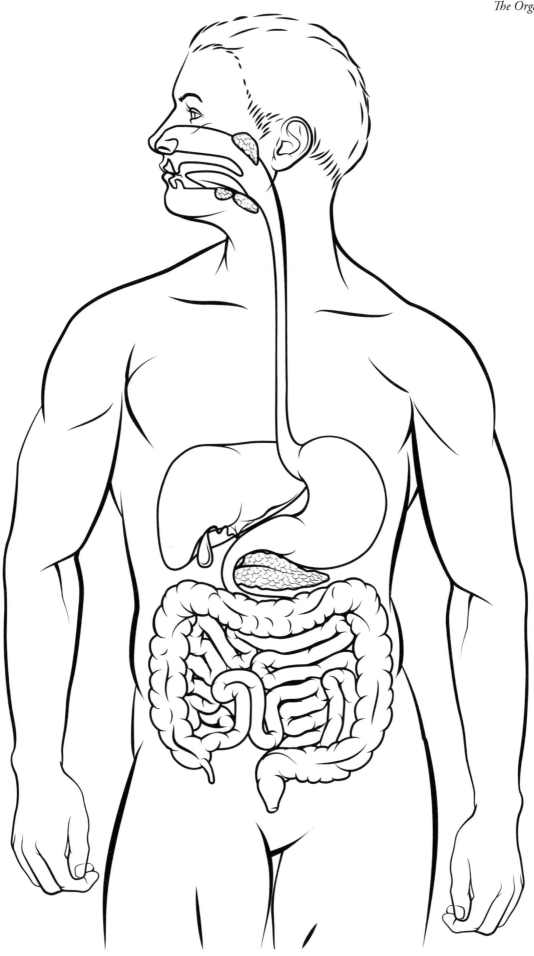

Skin

THE LAYERS OF SKIN

EPIDERMIS

DERMIS

SUBCUTANEOUS
TISSUE

MUSCLE

Jordan learned, the skin is the largest organ of your body. It is important to keep your skin clean. The skin keeps TOXINS, WASTE, GERMS, chemicals and unwanted material from entering your body. Taking a bath, makes you feel better.

Your skin protects your bones, inner organs and blood vessels. It breathes, needs water and oxygen. Your skin breathes!

The skin of people varies in color; brown, black, light brown, red, pale, white, tan.

Foods: cheese, milk, oil, eggs.

THE LAYERS OF SKIN

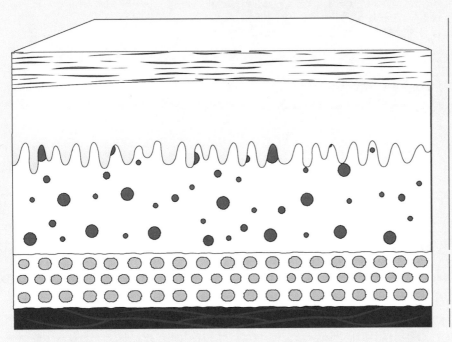

EPIDERMIS

DERMIS

SUBCUTANEOUS
TISSUE

MUSCLE

Systems

Digestive System

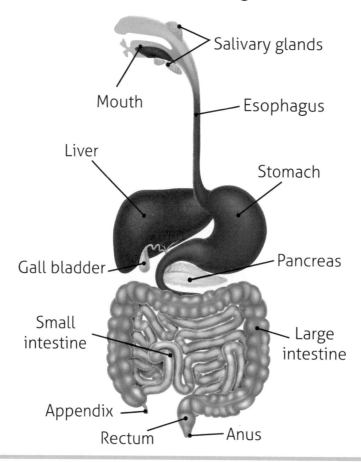

Salivary glands

Mouth

Esophagus

Liver

Stomach

Gall bladder

Pancreas

Small intestine

Large intestine

Appendix

Rectum

Anus

Jordan wanted to understand what happens when we eat and drink: When we eat food, it gets chewed up in your mouth. Once swallowed the food travels down your esophagus to the stomach.

From the stomach, food is broken down and makes its way through the colon. During this process, many other organs including the liver, gall bladder, pancreas become involved to further breakdown the food, absorb vitamins, minerals and nutrients to help you grow strong and tall. All the digestive organs work together as an orchestra.

Unused food makes its way to exit your body, then you must go number two. This is a normal part of everyday life and will help you stay healthy.

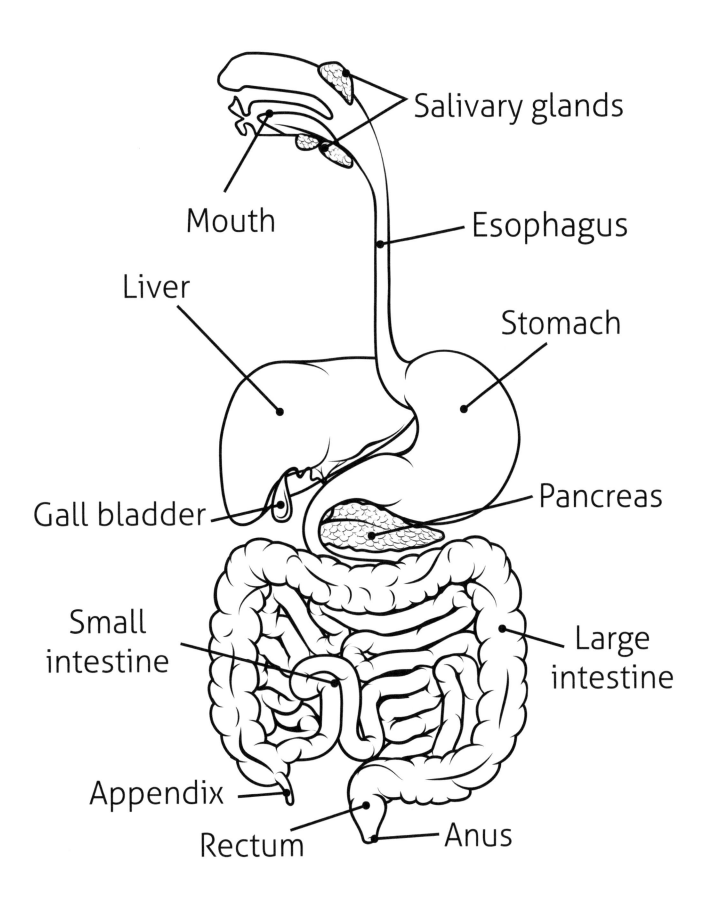

Salivary glands

Mouth

Esophagus

Liver

Stomach

Gall bladder

Pancreas

Small
intestine

Large
intestine

Appendix

Rectum

Anus

Musculoskeletal: Bones

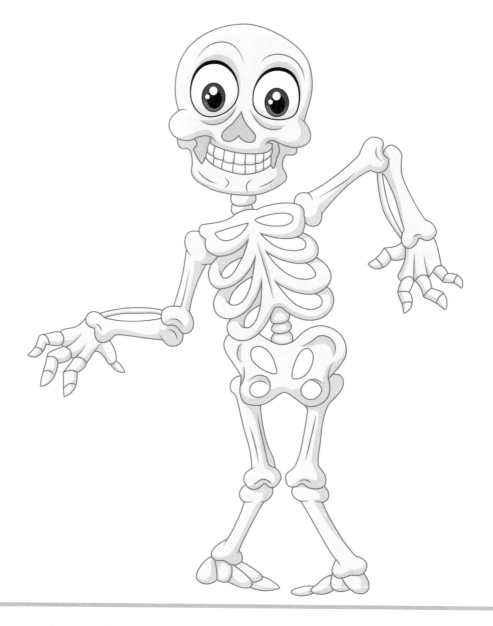

Jordan next learned about bones and how they protect our body: The bones are called a skeletal system which protects the inner organs of your body. They support, protect and allows you to move, dance and play. Bones also help produce red blood cells and they store calcium. Calcium is a mineral that keeps your bones strong.

Therefore, calcium rich foods are important to eat to keep your bones in good health. Dark green leafy vegetables, cheese, dairy, eggs, yogurt, almonds, fish (salmon).

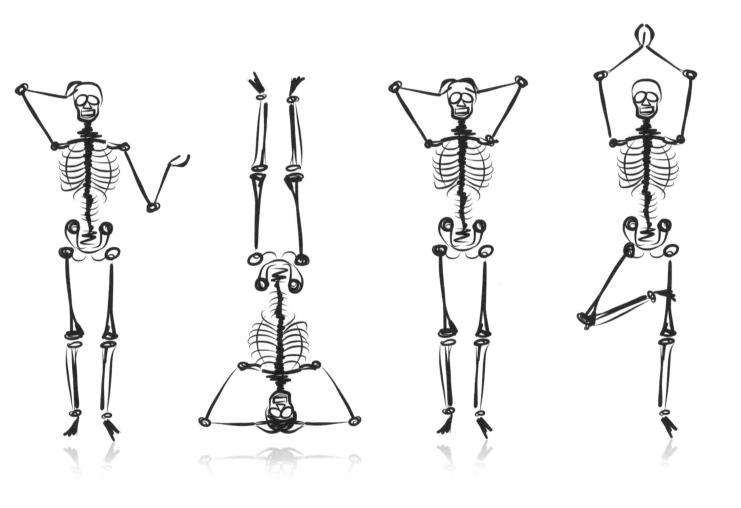

Circulatory System: Blood

Circulatory System for Kids

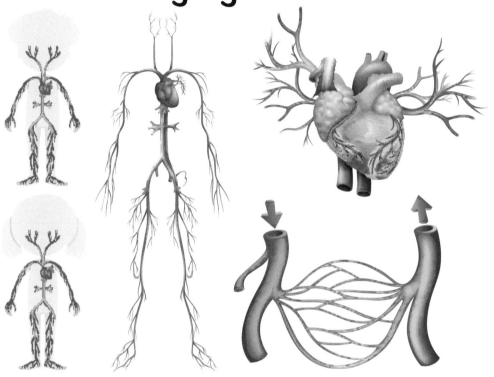

Blood keeps us alive.

How blood moves through our body was the next system Jordan learned about. Blood is made in the bones and the spleen. It is a fluid influenced by the food and water you drink. It is important to eat healthy foods to avoid getting sick. The heart pumps blood through your entire body.

Eggs are good to keep blood vessels strong.

It is said, during an average lifetime, the heart will pump about 1.5 million barrels of blood which equivalent to about 200 train cars. (Chandrahas Hawaldar: Quora- January 29, 2015, India)

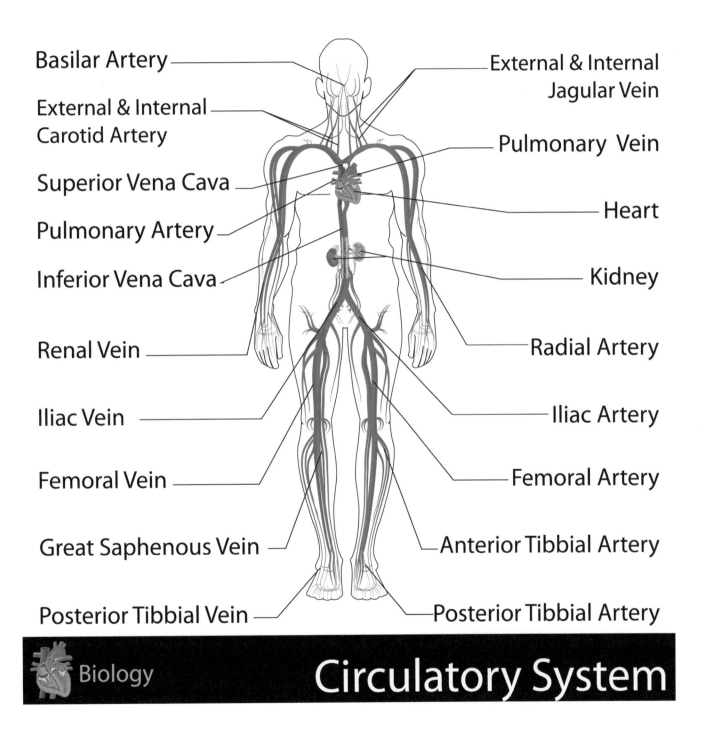

Basilar Artery

External & Internal Carotid Artery

Superior Vena Cava

Pulmonary Artery

Inferior Vena Cava

Renal Vein

Iliac Vein

Femoral Vein

Great Saphenous Vein

Posterior Tibbial Vein

External & Internal Jagular Vein

Pulmonary Vein

Heart

Kidney

Radial Artery

Iliac Artery

Femoral Artery

Anterior Tibbial Artery

Posterior Tibbial Artery

Biology

Circulatory System

Foods to Stay Healthy and Strong

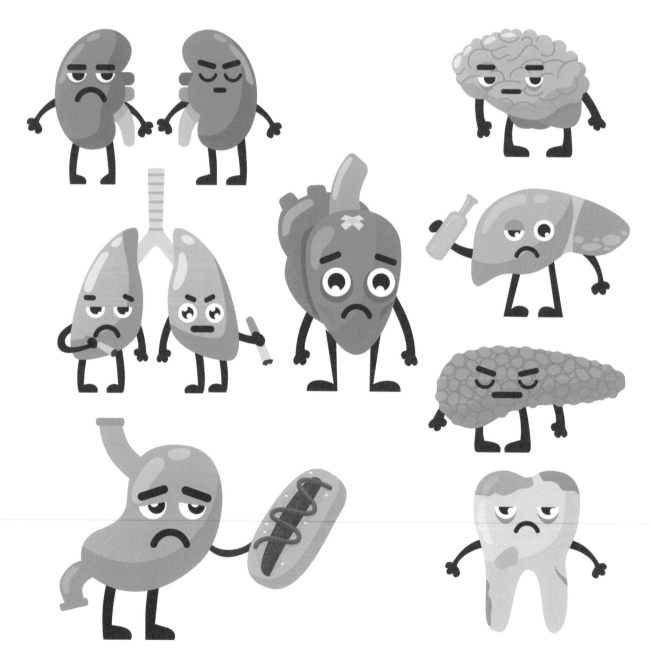

Vegetables to eat
for good health

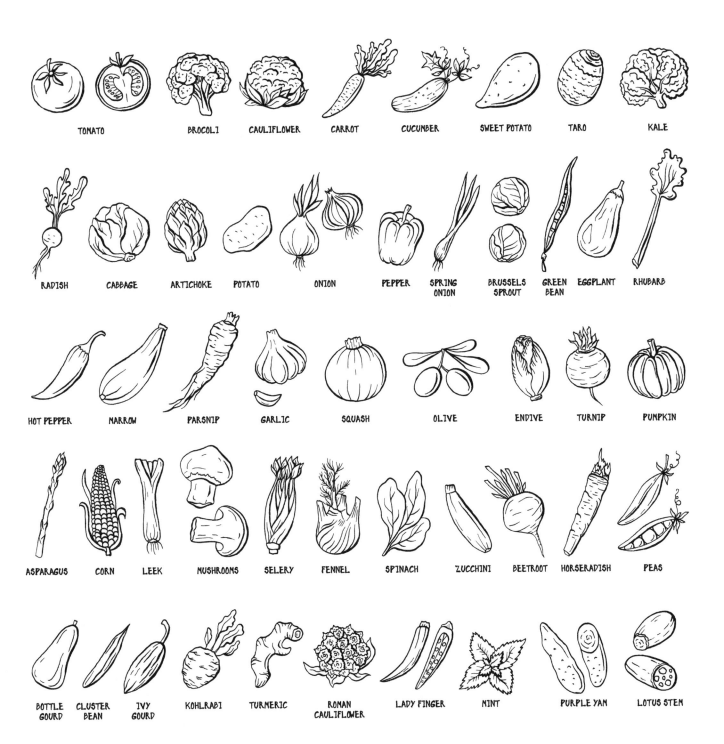

TOMATO • BROCOLI • CAULIFLOWER • CARROT • CUCUMBER • SWEET POTATO • TARO • KALE

RADISH • CABBAGE • ARTICHOKE • POTATO • ONION • PEPPER • SPRING ONION • BRUSSELS SPROUT • GREEN BEAN • EGGPLANT • RHUBARB

HOT PEPPER • MARROW • PARSNIP • GARLIC • SQUASH • OLIVE • ENDIVE • TURNIP • PUMPKIN

ASPARAGUS • CORN • LEEK • MUSHROOMS • SELERY • FENNEL • SPINACH • ZUCCHINI • BEETROOT • HORSERADISH • PEAS

BOTTLE GOURD • CLUSTER BEAN • IVY GOURD • KOHLRABI • TURMERIC • ROMAN CAULIFLOWER • LADY FINGER • MINT • PURPLE YAM • LOTUS STEM

Fruits to eat for good health

Watermelon   Melon   Pineapple   Coconut

Banana   Apple   Pomegranate   Passionfruit   Avocado

Pear   Lemon   Orange   Apricot   Mandarin   Kiwi

Peach   Plum   Grapes   Sea buckthorn   Currant   Berberis

Gooseberry   Cowberry   Blueberry   Cranberry   Raspberry   Strawberry   Cherry

Meat, Poultry and Fish

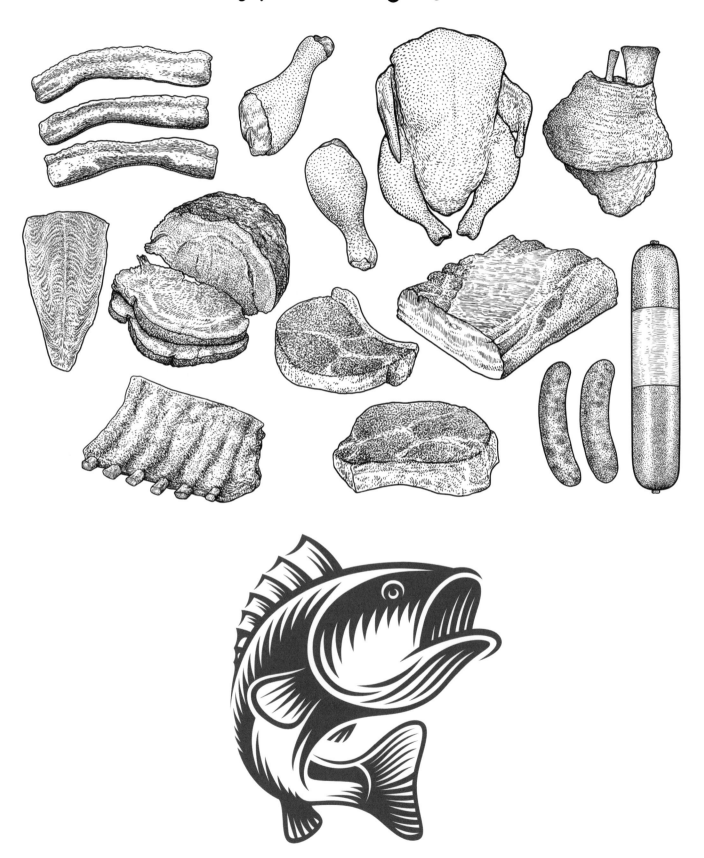

43

After months of getting the sleep needed, reading about the body and eating food needed to be healthier, Jordan could outplay mom every day, made new friends and did excellent in school!

Jordan got better!

Children of the world come in different colors; brown, dark brown, red, yellowish white, white, tan.

They also have different colors of hair, eyes and different languages.

Color your friends in different shades.

Jordan thanks you for reading this story and hopes you will keep the <u>"Organ Project"</u> forever! (Which Jordan are you?)

Other Works by Renee Grace

Under One Olive Tree:

www.authorhouse.com

ISBN 10: 150490298X soft cover; ISBN 13: 9781504902984 hard cover:

STREETS OF GOLD JEWELS ®

Mission – *Deliver quality, customized, affordable signature jewelry as a pie ce of art.*

Vision – *Every Queen of the Earth have a customized mothers' or birthstone bracelet or necklace made exclusively for her. Present the city of the New Jerusalem as art in jewelry. (Rev. 21: 18)*

Philosophy of Life – *Work hard, play hard, live a healthy, happy life and bless as many people possible along the way. Isaiah 29: 12: "All that we have accomplished He has done for us."*

Jewelry line:

1. New Jerusalem Jewelry: Streets of Gold Jewels

2. Mothers' bracelets and necklaces at request:

3. Rainbow bracelets and necklaces at request.

Primary stones used: Fresh Water Pearls and Swarovski Pearls. Birthstone Swarovski Crystals; Gemstones.

New Jerusalem Jewelry: Streets of Gold Jewels ®

Origin: Revelation 21: 18-21(NIV)

18 The wall was made of jasper, and the city of pure gold, as pure as glass. 19 The foundations of the city walls were decorated with every kind of precious stone.

The first foundation was jasper, the second sapphire,

the third agate, the fourth emerald, 20 the fifth onyx, the

sixth ruby, the seventh chrysolite, the eighth beryl, the

ninth topaz, the tenth turquoise, the eleventh jacinth,

and the twelfth amethyst.21 The twelve gates were

twelve pearls, each gate made of a single pearl.

The great street of the city was of gold,

as pure as transparent glass.

Each New Jerusalem piece:

12 pearls with at least one stone of:

Jasper

Chrysoprase

Sapphire

Chalcedony

Emerald

Amethyst

Beryl

Sardonyx

Chrysolite/ Peridot

Carnelian

Topaz

Jacinth

Mothers' bracelets/birthstone

Jan- Garnet

Feb- Amethyst

March- Aquamarine

April- Diamond

May- Emerald

June- Alexandrite/Pearl

July- Ruby

August- Peridot

Sept- Sapphire

Oct- Opal

Nov- Topaz

Dec- Tanzanite/Tourquoise

Rainbow Line:

Bracelets and Necklaces made from Swarovski crystals:

Buyer may choose silver or gold base

as well as both if requested.

Red

Orange

Yellow

Green

Blue

Indigo

Violet

Proprietor and originator of Trademark:

Renee Grace (AKA)

"Streets of Gold Jewels® *is officially Trademarked by the USPTO."*

Renee Grace grew up in the Metropolitan area of Detroit,

Michigan and has been an RN over 25 years.

Renee Grace is her signature name for Trademarked handmade

jewelry called Streets of Gold Jewels®.

It can be found on Etsy.com under store name:

StreetsofGoldJewels

Email: reneesog@yahoo.com

Author Bio

(AKA)- Renee Grace- (birth name identified at the end of the book, Under One Olive Tree); born in Mt. Clemens, North-East Metropolitan area of Detroit, Michigan. She attended private elementary and secondary education.

Formal education:

Western Michigan University: Kalamazoo, MI; Health Ed and Business ,1982:

Kellogg Community College: Battle Creek, MI; Nursing, 1991 and 1994:

International College (Hodges University): Naples, Florida; Master's in Business Administration (MBA), Cum Laude, December 2006:

Elite Education, Robert Kiyosaki founder: (Remote Business School); 2015- lifelong learning:

As a Professional Nurse - RN 25+ years, achieved certifications in Rehabilitation Nursing and Professional Healthcare Management, and an MBA (Cum Laude). Renee has worked and lived in 12 states.

Tenures in Nursing practice: Rehabilitation and Acute patient care x 14 years, Corporate Nursing, Travel Nursing and Insurance. Worked contract for The United States Air Force (USAF), 3+ years as a Utilization Manager spearheading different venues of projects, then as a Medical Report Writer.

Renee has been a member of Association of Rehabilitation Nurses; Toastmasters Member and Speaker; Volunteer for Barn Buddies Rescue Mission Farm/ The Farm, in Las Vegas, NV.

Renee has also done a myriad of Volunteer Medical Mission short term assignments in Ecuador, Zambia, Peru, Haiti, N. Carolina, Israel and Burkina Faso, NW Africa. Has traveled overseas 35+ times in her lifetime for these trips as well as to experience the world.

The highlight (fun) of all travel experiences was swimming in the "Devils Pool" which is a natural pool at the edge of Victoria Falls in Livingstone, Zambia.

Renee plans future sequalae's in time to continue Jordan's story; growing up, learning, developing childhood and bringing the family together.

Renee's heart, is that parent and caregivers move into your child; strengthen their strengths; instill curiosity into children re: their bodies, health and promote lifelong learning.

The Organ Project translation in Spanish available May 2018!

Printed in the United States
By Bookmasters